An indescribable loss ha
someone you love has d

You may feel a sense of unreality.
You may feel immersed in an unfathomable sea of shock.
You may want to howl … or hide.

While your personal world has irrevocably changed, the
outside world keeps turning.
You ask: 'How can others go on as normal? Don't they know?'
But no one knows exactly how you feel: your loss and grief
are unique.
You may feel like hugging this loss close to you, as you
search for comfort.

Yet there is only numbness.
Just for a while, this numbness is necessary.
It is the way your mind, body and emotions offer protection.

Be kind to yourself.

Step slowly and gently onto this pathway of grief.

These first days are not ordinary.
Yet ordinary things must still be done.

Simple tasks like eating, washing and attempting to sleep
may seem pointless, exhausting and difficult. Everything
takes so much longer.

Other people may seem distant. Sometimes it's just our
family we need close by. Share these days with those you love
and trust, but don't feel you have to shoulder their grief too.
Someone outside the family, who was less close to the
one who has died, may be able to help you most. Let them
share the practical tasks: registering the death or helping
you with financial matters.
They will remember details you might forget (grief can cause
absent-mindedness); they can help with form-
filling and simple decision-making. You can
leave big decisions until you are thinking
more clearly.

At a time like this,
busyness can be
a small blessing.

The Path Not Chosen

Beginning the Journey of Loss and Bereavement

Wendy Bray

WAVERLEY ABBEY
RESOURCES

In trying to help, people may tell you what you should do. Listen to their advice, do what helps you, and ignore the rest. Don't be persuaded to do what doesn't feel right. Be real: be *you*.

Telling the 'story' of your loss may alleviate the pain. If someone tries to stop you, tell them that it helps you to tell your story.

Others will say, 'Be strong.' You may try. But in trying to be strong we often camouflage our feelings. Don't hide your grief.

Walking the pathway of grief takes strength and determination. Just walk: at your own pace, in your own way. That, in itself, honours the one you have lost. Wouldn't they want you to be yourself?

'Even though I walk through
the valley of the shadow of death ...
you are with me ...'

Psalm 23:4

The funeral can be a *carrier* and a *catalyst*.

Organising it may *carry* you through the first days of grief.
The details occupy your mind, and the planning keeps
you busy.
Then the day arrives, and you have to cope with other
people: what they say; how they look; and their grief –
it seems to be shaken out on top of your own.

Planning 'What I'll do if …' with your family or friends
may give you some security. Arranging a room to escape
to; a way out of a painful conversation; having someone to
hold tight at a bewildering moment – all these may help you
to get through.

As a *catalyst*, the funeral marks your crossing into the no-man's-land of grief. Here, reality bites hard.

Most of your family and friends will leave soon afterwards. An unbearable emptiness takes their place, and you have to face it. A different life now appears, one that you hardly dare imagine: a life in which your loved one is no longer present. This may be the most difficult time of all.

More than ever now, it is important to be real about how you feel, with yourself and those around you. In the weeks ahead your honesty will enable you, and those you love, to move through this inhospitable place.

'Sorrow is no longer the islands
but the sea.'

Nicholas Wolterstorff[1]

In this no-man's-land you face the **everyday reality** of personal loss.

Your grief and pain are as unique as the person who has died, as deep as the love you felt for them: your grief is the other side of love.

Just now it is the 'neverness' that is so painful: facing the fact that he or she will never again sit with you; call your name; laugh or cry with you. There is an aching chasm that cannot be filled.

Your grief may seem deep and wordless: a yearning; a desire to cry out, or groan in despair. Allow yourself to do that – even as a prayer. John Bunyan said that 'the best prayers are more often groans than words'.[2] And St Paul assures us that the Holy Spirit 'intercedes' to turn our groans into prayers.

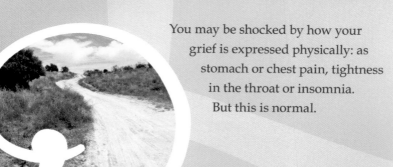

You may be shocked by how your grief is expressed physically: as stomach or chest pain, tightness in the throat or insomnia. But this is normal.

Acknowledge all that you have been through – and have yet to go through. Your body is worn down. It needs rest.

Don't do more than you feel able to. Lean on friends who are strong in empathy, gentle in action and honest in their words.

Know that while the moment of your loss may be etched in time, there is no time limit for its aftermath. The grief pathway winds on ahead. Tread slowly and gently, and take time to understand yourself.

'Come to me,
all you who are weary and burdened,
and I will give you rest.'

Matthew 11:28

The pathway of grief is a necessary one, leading to a future in which your loss can be remembered honourably, without pain.

There is no 'right' way through grief; no pre-determined route; no 'one size fits all' model.
Yours is a unique journey.

You may move between deep anxiety, denial and disbelief, and you will probably experience anger and depression – and return to each of these feelings again and again.

You will take steps forward – only to take more steps back. But that's OK.

Others may try to hurry you to 'the end', wanting resolution. Do not be hurried.

Grief is like finding a way through dense jungle with a machete. It is hard work: long, slow, exhausting, repetitive; involving the same effort, the same pain, over and over, moving you towards a clearing.

There is also a necessity to **the practicalities of loss**.
There are tasks that must be done: they may be the
hardest challenges you have ever attempted.

The harsh face of reality meets you as you deal with your
loved one's possessions.
Don't rush this. Wait until you feel strong enough to start,
and ask someone to help you.
Don't consider giving items away, or changing your
familiar surroundings, for some time to come.

Make big decisions carefully.

Maintain a dialogue about your feelings: with yourself, with
others – and with God, if praying helps you. Take time to
acknowledge and experience those feelings – don't try to switch
them off, turn them away, or bury them under your busyness.

Continue to be real.

'The LORD is close to the
broken-hearted ...'

Psalm 34:18

Tears are synonymous with grieving. They are one way in which we release sadness: a natural means of healing.

But not all of us respond to loss by crying: the absence of tears may not reflect the depth of our grief. Whether you cry or not may have more to do with your upbringing or personality than the nature of your loss. So, never feel that you 'should' cry; equally, never feel that you have to stop your tears, that you should 'pull yourself together' or keep 'a stiff upper lip'.

Tears are a natural, and often necessary, part of grief. Cry as and when, where and how, you want to. This is *your* grief.

Tears of grief can be unpredictable.

At times they are gut-wrenching, at other times they seem unending: perhaps these are the deepest and most healing of tears.

Often, much later, they fall unexpected, unbidden. You come across a forgotten article of clothing or a piece of handwriting; or you see something random on the street; and suddenly you are reminded of the loss that is always – will always be – there.

Welcome those tears, and take a moment to embrace the sadness.

Remember: tears can bring healing.

The tears streamed down …
and I let them flow freely as they would,
making of them a pillow for my heart.
On them it rested.

Augustine, *Confessions IX, 12*

Anger is almost always part of grief.

We feel anger at those we feel are 'responsible': at the one who has died, at God or at ourselves.

Your anger is normal, even necessary. It is a protest: this death seems unfair, wrong.

You are also raging in bitter frustration at your inability to 'bring back' the one you have lost.

It's OK to be angry and to express these frightening feelings – even your anger at God.

Anger needs both acknowledgement and expression. It needs to be 'put somewhere safe'.

Choose someone to whom you can, in some way, say: 'I need you to understand my anger, accept my rage and feel my fury.' Share their safe and comforting company for as long as it takes.

'Out of the depths I cry to you,
O LORD; O Lord, hear my voice.'

Psalm 130:1–2

In bereavement, our suffering screams 'No!' from every part of us.

Sometimes your scream may be a silent one, from the depths of **despair, withdrawal and isolation.**

Shunning company, you prefer to be alone, longing only to wrap yourself tightly in the black cloak of loss. You may experience a yearning, and perhaps a clear sense of living in 'the shadow of death'.

This loneliness may be worse several months into the grief journey. At this time, most support will have dropped away: everyone seems to have forgotten your bereavement, and you may be left feeling desolate.

Nothing reaches you except grief; nothing moves you except a sense of loss.

Gripped by despair, you face an almost unimaginable future without the person you love.

Feeling isolated is normal, for a while, even when friends and family are around trying to help. It *is* true that 'no one really understands' exactly what you are going through, even when they are also grieving.

But try not to shut yourself away from others for too long: shared sorrow and grief can lead us out of isolation and despair, into hope – especially through the sharing of happy memories.

While it is normal sometimes to feel 'no one really understands how I feel', it isn't normal to experience a continued, deep sense of isolation for weeks or months – or to constantly want your life to end.

'He has sent me to bind up
the broken-hearted …
to comfort all who mourn …'

Isaiah 61:1–2

If your feelings of isolation continue beyond 'a while', you might have become stuck or **lost on the grief pathway**; unable to move towards that 'clearing': the place of acceptance where you can live with your loss, and the feelings that go with it.

You may be subconsciously denying your loss, or painfully prolonging your grief, especially if the death was sudden or traumatic. If you have been busy with young children or other life demands, you may have delayed your grieving. Sometimes, past losses make a present loss more difficult. If you think this might apply to you, talk to a specialist bereavement counsellor.

There is a way through to the clearing: you just need someone to help you find the path again.

'The LORD will guide
you always ...'

Isaiah 58:11

As the grief journey continues you *will* **get through day by day**, although you will feel as though your life will never be the same. In many ways, that's true: a much-loved person will not now be part of your life in the same way.

Going back to work, laughing, enjoying activities, can mean that you feel guilty, as if going back to an enjoyable life betrays your love for the one who has died. These feelings are normal: but you need not feel guilty.

Remember that grief is 'the other side of love'. You have not lost everything about your loved one, nor are you forgetting them. They are still part of your life: you will carry them with you always.

You will have bad days and better days.

Some difficult days are expected: birthdays, wedding anniversaries ... and then the anniversary of the death.

Special occasions, like Christmas, will magnify your loss. The absence of the one with whom you want to share the day seems to steal the reason to celebrate – especially with others. As always, do what feels right to you, and don't be afraid to change your mind. Say yes to invitations, but make sure everyone knows that you might not be able to face the day after all.

Accept that these are the toughest times.

But be brave. Your fears may be unfounded, and you may enjoy moments of rediscovered joy.
Believe that, in time, you will once again find meaning in life and its milestones.

'I will turn their mourning into gladness;
I will give them comfort and joy
instead of sorrow.'

Jeremiah 31:13

Others say: 'Time will heal.'

At first, those words sting. 'How much time?!' you say.
Months later, your grief may seem worse – as if you are
'going backwards'.

But you may, eventually, see some truth in those words.

Moment by moment, you will find ways to adapt to the loss
of the world you knew, and the loss of the person you were.

You will find a place in this new and unfamiliar world.

The future, which at the very beginning of this journey is so
incomprehensible, is yours still.

You may never get over your loss, or find 'closure': we don't
shut the door on our losses. But you will learn
to hold your loss close to yourself –
with more comfort – and you will
journey forward with it.

Letting go is very hard.

But beyond the dark time of uncertainty and bewilderment there are always new beginnings.
These fresh starts are nurtured by – and wouldn't be possible without – what the loved one gave us.

Nothing can take away the life we have shared with our loved ones: they help to shape who we are and who we will be.

In the face of loss, we get in touch with our own suffering and resilience; we gain a panoramic view of the human condition, and tap into our own spiritual strength.

Often, through religious and spiritual belief we see order in chaos; we begin to make sense of life and death; and we maintain a continuing bond with the one we have lost.

'For I know the plans I have for you,'
declares the LORD,
'... plans to give you hope and a future.'

Jeremiah 29:11

Faith does not dispel tears, but it does change their nature: in God, faith gives us someone wise, loving and empathetic to share our grief with.

What we experience of God and others in the suffering of grief can strengthen our faith.
Meaning can be found in suffering, through our relationship with God. God knows what it is to suffer.[3]
The pathway of grief and suffering can build character and hope beyond the deep sadness.

All of us would rather go another way, but when there is no choice let us remember that this pathway of grief is 'soul-making'.

It is natural to want to find some connection with the one you have lost.

You 'search' for the one you love because the love remains.

How you search may depend on your idea of an afterlife. Christians believe in the promise of heaven: that God promises a resurrection of the body; that personal identity will be preserved in the joy of heaven.[4]

None of us know exactly what this means for those we have lost, but the assurance that God is loving, forgiving and gracious offers us hope.

This hope, along with our memories of, and our enduring love for, the one we have lost can bring us peace as we face the future. However you search, what you find will be love.

'And now these three remain:
faith, hope and love.
But the greatest of these is love.'

1 Corinthians 13:13

Grief takes us where we do not want to go,
and every second of it seems an eternity:
but it is a necessary journey.

At times you will share the path with others, but your way
is yours alone.

Each step, each turning point, every straining look ahead and
tearful look behind, each moment of wondering if the road will
ever end, is part of a journey of love for the one you have lost.

Be patient with yourself: find your own pace.

You *will* find comfort and you *will* find peace.

Eventually you will find meaning, and a new and stronger self.

Every ending, however heartbreaking, is always followed by a new beginning.

So, step slowly and gently on to this pathway of grief ...

'He will wipe every tear from their eyes.
There will be no more death
or mourning or crying or pain,
for the old order of things has passed away.'

Revelation 21:4

What might **help your walk** along the grief pathway?

It's important to express grief in some way. A wise friend or counsellor will help you with feelings that are difficult to cope with alone. If talking to those around you isn't easy, try writing a letter to the one who has died.

Perhaps you can absorb yourself in a creative task your loved one had planned: for example, planting a spring garden.

Spend time with a friend who can share something of your experience: shared routines like shopping can help, as well as talking and listening.

Don't be afraid to reminisce – and laugh – about your loved one with family and friends. It keeps their memory alive.

Bereavement support groups can help you cross the bridge back into 'the outside world' – even if you make forays to and fro for a while.

If reading will help you, try these books:

Wendy Bray and Diana Priest, *Insight into Bereavement* (Farnham: Waverley Abbey Resources, 2006).

Fiona Castle, *Rainbows Through the Rain*. A book of readings to accompany the grief journey (London: Hodder and Stoughton, 1999).

Tom Gordon, *New Journeys Now Begin: Learning on the path of grief and loss* (Glasgow: Wild Goose Publications, 2007).

Pablo Martinez and Ali Hull, *Tracing the Rainbow: Walking through loss and bereavement* (Carlisle: Authentic, 2004).

Nicholas Wolterstorff, *Lament for a Son* (Grand Rapids: Eerdmans, 1987).